# MASKS

## From Around the World

### A PERSONAL COLLECTION

Garth Dahl

**Library and Archives Canada Cataloguing in Publication**

Dahl, Garth, 1956-

Masks from around the world : a personal collection / Garth Dahl.

Includes bibliographical references.

ISBN 1-894694-45-7 (bound)
ISBN 1-894694-41-4 (pbk.)

I. Masks—Private collections—Catalogs. 2. Dahl, Garth, 1956-
—Ethnological collections—Catalogs. I. Title.

NK4890.M37D33 2006 731'.75074 C2006-902171-6

Editor: Graham Hayman
Proofreader: Neall Calvert
Book designer: Rebecca Davies
Mask photography: Alistair Eagle

First printing 2006

Printed in China

Granville Island Publishing
212–1656 Duranleau
Vancouver, BC, Canada V6H 3S4
Tel: (604) 688-0320 Toll free: 1-877-688-0320
www.GranvilleIslandPublishing.com

## Dedication

To Agnes, my loving wife, who I drag into every marketplace I see. I am happy that we share the joy of mask collecting. I value her opinions, and I was especially happy to have her with me in Haida Gwaii on our most recent journey to visit a mask maker.

I also dedicate this book to the God within me, who gives my life direction and purpose. He is the only one who sees me without my mask.

# Acknowledgements

I wish to thank the talented mask carvers worldwide for preserving the art of mask design, and for making their masks available to collectors.

Without the hospitality of the people from Haida Gwaii I would never have understood their culture; I thank them for allowing me into their world. To Reg Davidson, in particular, I am grateful; it was a pleasure being a guest in his studio. As I watched him carve he made it look easy, but his confidence comes from years of experience. That's what makes him one of the best.

And finally, Graham Hayman's resourcefulness as an editor was much appreciated.

# TABLE OF CONTENTS


**Introduction** vi

**Latin America** 1

Republic of Costa Rica 3

Cuba 8

Republic of Mexico 14

Brazil 18

**Africa** 20

Central Africa 22

West Africa 26

**Europe** 32

France 33

Greece 36

Czech Republic 38

Italy 40

**Pacific Rim** 42

Hawaii 44

Hong Kong 45

Japan 46

Thailand 48

British Columbia, Canada 52

Reconnection 63

Interview with Reg Davidson 65

The End of Mourning 69

**Conclusion** 74

**References** 75

# INTRODUCTION

I was compelled to write this book after I showed photographs of my masks to several schoolteachers, who said a book about masks would be of interest to their students. *Masks: A Personal Collection* is an introduction to the masks of the world and is intended for people who are curious about this centuries-old art form. I want to share the excitement of discovery I experienced collecting masks from all over the world.

It was in Mexico that I first became aware of the magic of masks. In 1989 I visited Playa del Carmen, a little town south of Cancún with dirt roads and few hotels, and ate at a seafood restaurant called Las Máscaras (The Masks). Hundreds of masks lined its walls, and I was amazed at the variety and workmanship of the masks collected by the owner during his years of travelling the world.

Inspired by his collection, I bought my first mask in Costa Rica. Now there are over one hundred masks covering the walls of a room in my home, most of them found on my travels throughout Asia, Central and South America and Europe. When I bought from local vendors, I usually learned something from them

about the history and cultural significance of these masks. In some instances, the artisans sold their masks directly to me and shared the masks' mythological meaning while discussing the materials used in creating these unique faces. Many cultures believe certain animals symbolize or express human qualities and that animal-like masks contain spiritual power and can ward off evil spirits or invite good luck, wealth and prosperity. Some of the most fascinating masks in my collection combine both human and animal characteristics.

Old masks are valuable treasures. In addition to their artistic significance, they represent the historic and cultural roots of many of the world's indigenous peoples. New masks also have value because they demonstrate how various cultures around the world have evolved over time. Today, many artisans carve masks for the tourist trade while others are creating masks as collectible works of art, to be displayed in homes, galleries, museums, in exhibitions and public spaces. Through travel and exposure to other artists and cultures, modern mask artists have discovered innovative ways to design and produce their work by utilizing new materials and incorporating fresh ideas into their masks.

These changes, along with global tourism and trade, have taken masks that are created in small villages to the marketplaces of large towns, from street vendors to wholesale exporters. I bought an African mask in a market in Thailand, for example, and a Brazilian mask on eBay, the Internet auction site.

The masks displayed in my home are quite new, made of modern materials and finished with oil paint, varnish and chemical glue. Some may not be made exactly like traditional masks, but after the style of old masks, combining elements of other cultures and artistic influences from around the world. Regardless of whether a mask

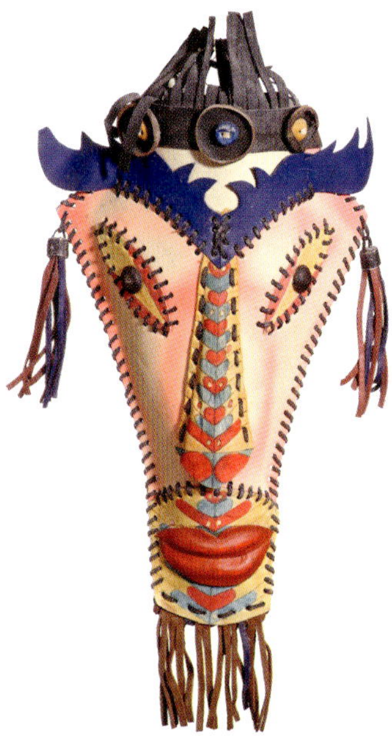

costs several dollars or several thousands of dollars, I appreciate and value the work of the artists.

I live near Vancouver, British Columbia, and used to travel frequently to countries in Asia, Europe and South America on business as well as vacation, but as my trips grew less frequent, I turned my attention to discovering masks closer to home. I found interesting masks throughout the province and learned about the wonderful masks crafted by people of First Nations ancestry. I read about the legends that inspired these masks, and found a strong desire among the First Nations to maintain and develop their traditional arts and culture.

It was through my interest in First Nations masks that I met Reg Davidson, the well-known Haida carver. He generously spoke to me about his work and shared his thoughts on mask carving and tribal customs. An invitation to visit his home in Haida Gwaii, more widely known as the Queen Charlotte Islands, led to my participating in an important ceremony in 2005. This ceremony, known as End of Mourning, marked a tremendous achievement by the First Nations people in preserving their history. I've included a chapter on Reg Davidson and the End of Mourning celebration in my book as a tribute to the thriving arts culture of our country's indigenous people.

This book is organized into sections based on where I bought my masks: geographical regions and then countries. You may notice that masks from neighbouring countries have similar characteristics and utilize the same materials. I've written brief overviews of the geography, history and people of the countries where I travelled, in order to provide some context in which to study the masks in terms of their cultural roots. Masks are designed to be eye-catching, and I made the decision to include only a little background information on them in order to focus attention on the visual appeal of the images, so beautifully captured in the photographs by Alistair Eagle. My masks have names: if a mask didn't have one when I bought it, I would give it a name that complemented its distinct features.

Masks affect me on a deep personal level—I believe they invite us to consider the significant aspects of our creative lives, our cultural history and our ties to communities worldwide. Each mask has its own message, its own story to tell. I hope my book, and my collection of masks, inspires you to view masks in new ways: as collectible treasures and as an opportunity to learn about cultures all over the world.

*— Garth Dahl*

# Guide to the Masks in the Introduction

### vii. THE HEALER'S CHILD

This mask comes from southern Brazil, where it is believed that the gemstones will ward off evil and bring its owners happiness and good will (compare with the similar but larger mask, "The Healer," on page 18).

Made of porongo gourd, fired clay, fibre, bamboo, quartz crystals, semi-precious stones

4.25" x 2.5" x 2"

Brazil

Bought on eBay

### viii. TEMPLE KEEPER

This mask is typical of the Mayan civilization, as represented by the archaeological site Chichén Itzá.

Made of fired clay

6.5" x 7" x 2"

Mexico

Bought in a marketplace, Chichén Itzá

### viii. FACE OF SUNSET

To me this depicts a celebration of the sun.

Made of painted melon and coconut shells

7.5" x 7" x 3"

Mexico

Bought in a marketplace, Cancún

### ix. CHEERFUL SUN

This little fellow must be happy because of the warmth of the Mediterranean sun.

Made of wood

Crete

6.5" x 4" x 2.5"

### ix. SMILING MOON

An impish-looking mask wearing an affectionate smile.

Made of wood

Crete

6" x 4" x 2"

### x. THE KISSER

With her red lips, this girl must be a kisser.

Made of wood

19.5" x 7" x 4"

Italy

Bought in a curio store, Qualicum Beach, BC

### x. LONG FACE

With this mask, I feel the artistry was in choosing the right dyes.

Made of painted leather

15" x 9" x 3.5"

Cuba

Bought in a market by the sea, Old Havana

### xi. EXPRESSIONLESS

No smile on this one.

Made of leather

12" x 7" x 2"

Cuba

Bought in the marketplace, Varadero

### xii. AVENGER OF NIGHTMARES

Protects our dreams while we sleep. The bones that make up mouth, eyelines and chin were taken from fish. The tattoo-like markings on the face are made by stones set into the wood.

Made of fish bones, feathers, stone, wood

14" x 7.5" x 2"

Brazil

Bought on eBay

Let the journey begin...

# LATIN AMERICA

Central and South American countries attract Canadian and American tourists because they offer both a warm climate and a warm welcome. Like many Canadians, I've visited several Latin American countries.

Archaeological exploration of the Aztec and Inca empires has been popularized in many movies, and a visit to the ruins in this area would awaken the Indiana Jones in the least adventurous of us. By that I mean a desire to rediscover this world of popular legend and to collect reproductions of cultural artifacts.

Masks from this region usually have bright colours, and the features reflect the African influence imported during the era of slavery. You might want to compare these masks to the ones in the African section.

**MYSTERY WITH ENCHANTMENT**

This is the first mask I purchased. It reminded me of the figureheads on the prows of sailing ships. It looked carved, but proved on closer inspection to be formed from leather.

Made of leather

25" x 28" x 6"

Bought in marketplace, San José

# Costa Rica

The beauty of this land and its enchanting ecology are to be treasured. It was here that I actually began collecting masks.

The first European explorer to encounter Costa Rica was Christopher Columbus, in September 1502. He named it for its "rich coast." But civilization existed in Costa Rica long before he arrived, and signs of human occupation date back 10,000 years.[3]

When Columbus arrived, there were four major native tribes. None of these peoples survived as landowners after the arrival of the Spanish. Some died from the smallpox brought by the colonizers, some were enslaved, and some ran away to the mountains. Their descendants remain there, making up only one percent of the population.[4]

These masks represent the influences of the African, Chinese, Mexican and Spanish cultures. Several of the masks described below are from the Boruca tribe, who use each mask only once ceremonially, then sell it.[5]

Population: 3.8 million

Capital city: San José

People and Origins: Spanish, African, indigenous Indians, Chinese

Languages: Spanish, Creole English, Indian dialects[2]

**SLEEPY MEDICINE MAN**

This mask comes from a tribe in the Telemanca Mountains. I believe it is the image of the medicine man.

Made of painted fired clay and feathers

8" x 2" x 2" (excluding feathers)

A gift

**PARROT TWINS**

The Boruca carver of this mask used a form of camouflage: the observer's attention is diverted to the brighter bird images, yet there is a face visible.

Made of painted balsa wood

13" x 6.75" x 3.5"

Bought in marketplace,
San José

**WISE OWL**

Also from a Boruca maker. The owl's wide-eyed look attracts attention while the wearer peeps through eye slits in the lower mask.

Made of painted balsa wood

12.5" x 5" x 4"

Bought in marketplace,
San José

**DUAL PERSONALITIES**

I like how the faces seem distorted, as though they were pushing into new dimensions. The faces look Middle Eastern to me, which adds mystery.

Made of leather

21" x 14" x 6"

Bought in marketplace, San José

**CAMOUFLAGED CHIEF**

I imagine this mask, again from the Boruca tribe, would be worn by a chief or elder.

Made of painted balsa wood

14.5" x 8" x 3.5"

Bought in marketplace, San José

**SNAKES OF DECEPTION**

An unusually dark Borucan mask, depicting two serpent heads.

Made of painted balsa wood

14" x 6.5" x 3.75"

A gift from my brother David

**STOGIE PUFFER**

Cuba is famous for its cigars, so as a memento I wanted this mask showing a local with a stogie.

Made of painted plaster

12" x 8" x 3"

Bought in a market by the sea, Old Havana

# Cuba

This land of coffee, rum, cigars, white sandy beaches and vigorous Latin music, not to mention the charm of Old Havana, appeals to me. And I find it fascinating that communism exists 90 miles from the United States.

When Columbus saw Cuba on his first voyage in 1492, he is reported to have said, "This is the most beautiful land my eyes have ever seen." The word Cuba may simply mean "land," in the Arawak language of the Taíno.[7] The Taíno people were conquered and the island colonized by the Spaniards in the 1500s.

Cuba's history of conflict continued when Havana fell to the British in 1762. It remained occupied during the colonial wars between Britain, France and Spain. Spain recovered Cuba from the British a year later in exchange for other territories.[8]

The colonial history of Cuba was heavily influenced by the world market for sugar.[9] Spain lost interest in Cuba during the 1800s due to there being neither enough land nor enough slave labour to meet its commercial needs. However, in response to demand from the United States, Cuban plantations were expanded and bartering of African slaves to the island was vastly increased.

Population: 11 million

Capital city: Havana

People and Origins: Spanish, African, Chinese

Language: Spanish[6]

**THE PROUD CHIEF**

I am sure a North American native like this was never seen in Cuba, but I had to have it!

Made of deerskin and feathers

31" x 19" x 12"

Bought in Varadero

Cuba's independence from Spain and freedom for its slaves came simultaneously. The now famous Carlos Manuel de Céspedes, a plantation owner, freed his slaves in 1868. His revolutionary cry "Independence or Death!" started a ten-year conflict that united Cubans against the Spanish rule, and today the words are still close to Cubans' hearts. I saw them written everywhere, even on the sides of buildings.[10]

After hearing a lot about Cuba, I wanted to discover how life is different in a communist environment. I saw that there are certainly restrictions on freedom. However, people in Cuba know where they stand and what is permitted. People in the industrialized democracies appear to have many freedoms, but not everything is as it seems: there are many contradictions and a lot of propaganda!

Despite restrictions, Cubans display their artistic abilities in their music and art. My wife, Agnes, and I had a lot of fun getting to know the locals, and have returned to Cuba many times.

In 1999 I was walking with friends on Varadero Beach on a sweltering hot day and we needed some shade, so the covered market stalls were inviting. Everything from blankets and tablecloths to cigars and masks was for sale. In the last aisle, a vendor displayed a mask clearly inspired by North American sources, which I called "The Proud Chief" (left). It looked very much out of place, like a Hawaiian hula doll would in Alaska. Varadero was probably one of the strangest places to find a mask like that. I doubt that I will ever see one like it again.

Later, walking on the beach, I'm sure I was quite a sight in shorts holding the 31-inch buckskin mask. All eyes turned to view my new companion. It was so big it would fit only in a hockey bag, and that's how I brought it home.

Several other masks from Cuba were bought in a wonderful marketplace, teeming with the excitement of life, by the sea in Old Havana.

**SHAPED FACE**

A strong design composed of basic shapes: triangles, circles and squared elements.

Made of fired clay, painted

7.5" x 4.5" x 2"

Bought in a flea market, Langley,BC

**WITCH DOCTOR**

The face on this mask seems camouflaged with leaf designs.

Made of fired clay, painted

10" x 7" x 2"

Bought in Old Havana

**NATIVE MOMMA**

The vendor in Old Havana who sold me this mask looked strangely like the mask herself. Maybe she was the model.

Made of painted plaster

11" x 6" x 3"

Bought in Old Havana

**FEATHERS & 'STACHE**

The angle of the eyes adds to this mask's character.

Made of feathers, painted leather

14.5" x 6.5" x 1.5"

Bought in a market by the sea, Old Havana

**AZTEC PRIEST**

This eerie mask captures the spirit of Chichén Itzá. The sun slants over the pyramid, and the slithering snake travels toward the sacrificial pool. On both sides there are drops of blood.

Made of fired clay and glazed

12" x 7.5" x 4"

Bought in a shop in Cancún

# Mexico

This vast country is comprised of nearly two million square miles of desert, rainforest, mountains and fertile plains.

## The Aztec Period in Mexico

At the time of the Spanish conquest, various groups like the Mexica, Culhua, Tepanec and Tenochca were living in central Mexico. All claimed descent from the original "Aztlan" or Aztecs, a term now used collectively for all of them.

According to myth, the original Aztecs left "Aztlan" around the 12th century.[12] From the 14th century the Aztec empire expanded and it was still growing when the Spaniards arrived. The capital, Tenochtitlán, was the centre of civilization in Central America.[13] How the Aztecs, believing in a divine destiny, rose to imperial status within a century is a spectacular chronicle of political conflict and alliance.[14]

The Mexican masks I've collected through the years remind me of this history. As many tourists know, the prices quoted in street markets are more like challenges to the buyer's negotiating skills, invitations to haggle, than final hard prices. We discovered this practice in a shop in Cancún. My wife liked the design of a mask, so she asked the price. Claiming it was "very rare," the vendor said $400. We thought we knew the true value and persuaded him to sell it for much less.

Population: 100 million

Capital city: Mexico City

People and Origins: Mestizo (European and Amerindian descent), Amerindian (including Nahua, Maya, Zapotecs, Mixtecs, Totonacs and Tarascos or Purépecha)

Languages: Spanish and 59 indigenous languages[11]

**STONE FACED**

A face of mother-of-pearl makes this a rare, perhaps unique, design. The edging is of cut stones, notably jade and onyx. I use a candle to light it from behind: the glow gives it a surreal look.

Made of mother of pearl, cut stones, plaster

14" x 11.5" x 3"

Bought from a beach vendor, Puerto Vallarta

**STRAW MAN**

This mask is traditionally used during Halloween. Unusual as it may seem, straw masks have a connection to Ireland. In County Mayo, the "straw-boys," wearing masks, visit the bride's home on the wedding eve and dance with the bride and other girls.

Made of straw

26" x 9" x 3" (including the hair)

Bought in a marketplace, Cancún

**THE HEALER**

This mask's presence comes from its quartz crystals and semiprecious stones, which are thought to possess metaphysical powers. The amethyst (druze)[17] in the forehead symbolizes the "third eye" of wisdom.[18] It is believed that the gemstone mask will ward off evil and bring its owners happiness and goodwill.

Made of gourd, fired clay, fibre, bamboo, quartz crystals, semiprecious stones

14" x 9" x 7"

Bought in an art store, Harrison Hot Springs, BC

# Brazil

The basin of the Amazon River and its tributaries covers almost half of Brazil's territory. The region comprises one of the world's largest rainforest ecologies and is home to many of Brazil's indigenous Indian tribes. This balanced ecological system is the source of numerous medicines and natural plant-based remedies. The vast forest acts like lungs to supplement global oxygenation—now in a perilous state.

Brazil was ruled as a colony by Portugal for 300 years until independence in 1822. The largest and most populous country in South America, Brazil is a regional leader and South America's leading economic power. Its industrial and agricultural sectors are growing, and the interior is being developed.[16]

I have not visited Brazil. I bought one Brazilian mask from a dealer in Harrison Hot Springs in southern BC, near my home town. The owner collects unique objects from around the globe. I bought the other two (see Introduction) on eBay, as I have done with some of my other masks. Buying on eBay is not the most reliable way, but if you already have some knowledge of masks and know what to look for, and if you get more details and pictures from the seller, you can assess how rare it is. Then you can decide whether a mask is worth its price and has a place in your collection—but I would not have bought this way when I started out.

Population: 172 million

Capital city: Brasília

People and Origins: European, mulatto, African, Japanese, Amerindian

Languages: Portuguese, indigenous languages, Spanish, English and French[15]

# AFRICA

This continent, earth's second-largest land mass, contains more nations than any other continent. Man's oldest known ancestors lived here, and empires rose and fell thousands of years before the European powers began their colonizing. Despite the spread of writing, roads, cities and industry, some precolonial culture remains. Like me, most people think of animals first when they think of Africa, but collecting masks made me aware of Africa's cultural sophistication and diversity.[19]

Masks can be traced back thousands of years in Africa. They help us to better understand African culture. They are still made by hand with materials such as iron, clay, leather, fabric and different types of wood.

Traditional African masks are worn in different ways: on the face, as a covering for the entire head, or in some cases even on the back of the head. Some masks are so big they are worn on the shoulders and cover the body.

In Africa as elsewhere, masks are worn in religious and other rituals, during celebrations and initiations, for weddings and funerals—and in war. The person wearing the mask would sometimes go into a deep trance and during this time "communicate" with the spirit of a "being" or an "ancestor." The masked dancer would then pronounce messages of wisdom, and these needed translating by a tribal wise man.

There was a time when these ceremonies with masks were more common, but because of the modern, mobile Western lifestyle spreading through Africa, such traditions are being lost. Many masks are now made for the tourist trade, and not for ritual. Mask makers are moving between countries, learning new styles and methods. Consequently, we can no longer be certain what tribe or culture a recently carved mask comes from. For example, many carvers moved to the Ivory Coast because that country (during periods of peace) is a convenient place from which to export their crafts in containers.

**BLACK BEAUTY**

The facial features and head covering suggest it may be from an area in Africa where Arab influence is stronger.

Made of fired clay

9.5" x 6" x 2"

A gift from my sister-in-law Orsolya

My African masks were bought outside Africa (a continent I have still to visit), most of them in various stores near my home town in Canada. There is a characteristic African look that is virtually unmistakable. The Ghanaian masks were labelled on the back, and their standardized format suggests that many masker makers in Ghana have organized their output for export. The others were not labelled, but are probably from Central Africa. Several experts I consulted, who have either lived in Africa or have studied African culture, were unable to say with certainty where they come from. So I have grouped masks in the regions of Central and West Africa unless I am sure of their origins.

# Central Africa

This is a vast region straddling the Equator, running roughly from the tropic of Capricorn in the south to 15 degrees north of the Equator. On the west coast lie Namibia, Angola, the Democratic Republic of Congo, the Republic of the Congo, Equatorial Guinea, Gabon and Cameroon. The landlocked Central African Republic lies adjacent to Ethiopia on the east coast. Lying to the south are Tanzania, Kenya and Mozambique. Inland from north to south are Uganda, Rwanda, Burundi, Zambia, Malawi and Zimbabwe.

Rich mineral and oil deposits and ethnic differences have added to longstanding conflicts in the region. These conflicts have caused huge migrations that disturb culture and customs. Toward the south there is the threat of famine, due to poor rainfall and government land policies. AIDS and malaria claim thousands of lives. In a few places, mainly on the east coast, political stability has permitted economic development.

The Two-Headed Swordsman mask, a gift from a Cuban doctor friend of mine, came with some history. My friend worked in a hospital in a small South African village; he took a trip north to Zambia and bought this mask in the town of Kitwe in 1996. It is interesting to note that Cuba has had a strong connection to Africa since the time of slavery. African influences are still visible in the masks from Cuba, and connections between Cuba and South Africa continue in the present. To assist in providing health services equally for the whole population, Cuba sent many doctors to South Africa. Hence the path of this mask from Zambia to me!

**HARMONY WITH ELEPHANT**

The elephant motif is common in masks from Malawi.[20]

Made of African teak

10.5" x 5" x 2"

Bought in a home-fashions chain store, Langley, BC

**TWO-TONED**

This sombre-looking mask's eyes and lips have subtle two-tone colours and detail.

Made of painted wood

20" x 6.5" x 3"

A gift from my step-daughter Kristina, Langley, BC

**TWO-HEADED SWORDSMAN**

The swords in this beautiful, large, hardwood mask are removable. The oval shape is typical of southern African warrior shields.

Made of African teak

32.5" x 6" x 3"

A gift from Lewis, a Cuban doctor friend, who bought it in Zambia

**LADY OF HONOUR**

This appears to be a woman of distinction.

Made of wood

16" x 8" x 4"

Bought in a craft market, Cloverdale, BC

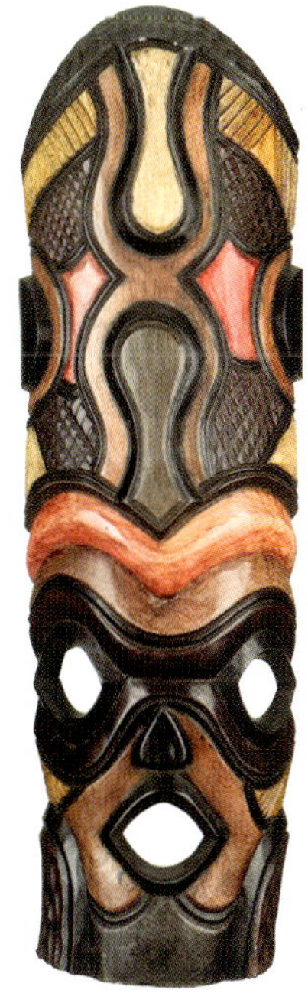

**SURPRISED**

The shaped designs on this mask give the face an expression of surprise. The elaborate headdress takes attention away from the facial area.

Made of painted wood

24" x 7.5" x 3"

Bought in a chain store, Langley, BC

**HANDLE MASK**

The stylized bearded chin might be a second handle, allowing the user to rapidly cover and uncover the face.

Made of painted wood

22" x 5" x 5"

Bought in a craft market, Cloverdale, BC

# West Africa

## Ghana

Ghana, well-endowed with natural resources, has an economy with roughly twice the output per person of the poorer countries in West Africa. The West has long been fascinated by the history of Ghana because of its central role in the gold, ivory and slave trades when the Ashanti empire was at its height.

The empire of the Ashanti people grew during the late 17th century and continued to prosper during the 18th-century slave trade. The capital, Kumasi, was then one of the most advanced cities in Africa. Many European individuals worked for the government as advisors and administrators. As colonizers, European countries built forts along the coastline, anchoring their trade in gold, ivory and slaves. It was known as the Gold Coast by the British, who considered it their own trading territory in the latter half of the 19th century. Total British domination was not achieved until 1900, when they defeated the Ashanti and the area's other strong kingdoms.[22]

**PROTECTOR OF BIRDS**

The bird appears at rest on the head of the image.

Made of wood

30" x 5.5" x 2.5"

Bought in a flea market, Cloverdale, BC

Population: 19.7 million

Capital city: Accra

People and Origins: Akan, Mole-Dagbane, Ewé, Ga, Guan, Gurma, Gonja, Dagomba

Languages: English, Ewé, Ga and Twi[21]

**BIRD BRAIN**

The rounded mouth on this mask shows surprise. Maybe it's a result of his new friend's beak piercing his forehead?

Made of wood and fabric

19" x 8" x 4"

Bought in a curio store, Qualicum, BC

**THINKING GECKO**

Can you find the twin geckos on the forehead?

Made of wood, mother of pearl

19" x 9" x 3.5"

A gift from Murray, a friend in BC

**DUAL WARRIORS**

I discovered the two figures in the forehead area after I had hung this mask on my wall. Many intricate details go unnoticed at purchase time, but when displayed they seem to stand out. Maybe masks just need more time to be examined.

Made of wood

8" x 6" x 2"

Bought in a market, Thailand

**THINKING WITH THE HEART**

This mask appears female because of the long earlobes or maybe earrings. Is love on her mind? Purchased in Thailand yet made in Ghana, this mask was obviously exported, so you might find a similar one at your local market.

Made of wood

9.5" x 5" x 2"

Bought in a market, Thailand

**HEAD IN THE AIR**

Giraffes, the world's tallest mammals, have small "horns" about five inches long on top of their heads. They are used to protect the head in fights.

Made of wood

14" x 5" x 2"

Bought in a curio store, Langley, BC

**ZIPPER**

The twin dotted lines on this mask remind me of zippers.

Made of wood

8" x 5" x 2"

Bought in Bangkok night market

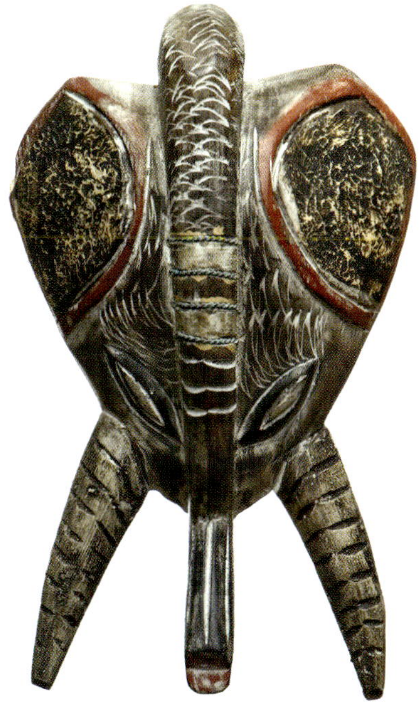

**TWO TUSKS AND A TRUNK**

The elephant is a symbol of strength. This mask shows the pachyderm in a slightly different way. Many have told me that this mask looks like an alien; maybe it's an alien elephant.

Made of wood

12" x 8" x 3.5"

A gift from my brother Greg

L'ARMEE FRANCAISE EMBARQUEE A BOULOGNE MENACAIT L'ANGLETERRE
UNE TROISIEME COALITION ECLATE SUR LE CONTINENT
LES FRANCAIS VOLENT DE L'OCEAN AU DANUBE
LA BAVIERE EST DELIVREE L'ARMEE AUTRICHIENNE PRISONNIERE A ULM
NAPOLEON ENTRE DANS VIENNE IL TRIOMPHE A AUSTERLITZ
EN MOINS DE CENT JOURS LA COALITION EST DISSOUTE

# EUROPE

My travels in Europe have focused on France, the Czech Republic, Greece and Italy. Today's Europe is very accessible. The border queues, passport stamps, uniforms, searches and charges of the past have been virtually eliminated. The traveller experiences great freedom and few delays across the borderless European Union.

## France

France is one of the world's most modern countries and a leader among the European nations. The mere name of Paris simultaneously evokes thoughts of romance and cultural sophistication. France has long been a world power and cultural leader, a dominant nation-state. Its global influence has been significant, not least because of its defining revolution of 1789. France once had many colonial possessions, but all that remain are small Pacific and Caribbean colonies. France paid a high price in two World Wars, and fought damaging colonial wars in the 1950s. Since then it has had periods of stability, with

**ARISTOCRAT**

With some imagination, you can see the two masks on this page at a ball for aristocrats in the France of days gone by.

Made of papier mâché

19" x 8" x 3"

Bought in an antique store, Surrey, BC

**FRENCH MAIDEN**

This could be the gentleman's mate. I liked the subtle mood on the faces that was captured by the artistic team of Micheline Larose and Georges Gamache.

Made of papier mâché

22.5" x 7" x 3"

Bought in an antique store, Surrey, BC

some notable exceptions like the 1968 riots by workers and students, and in 2005 the violent protests of dissatisfied Muslim immigrants from the former colonies.[24]

My friend Steve Jay and I travelled through France in May, the perfect time to see Europe—not too many other tourists blocking the views. We spent three days in and around Paris. Then by train we passed through the rest of France, Germany, Switzerland, Belgium, Austria and Italy, seeing the places most important to us.

Visiting the Louvre was like walking back in time. The preservation of antiquities is astonishing. I asked a guide about an Egyptian statue so flawless I thought it might be a reproduction. She said it was over 4,000 years old and assured me that everything I was viewing was original. At that moment I saw the museum and its artifacts in a new way. It influenced my view of masks—when you know their age and the effort that goes into making them, you see them differently.

I did not buy any masks on this trip. Perhaps I was not looking for them; I've discovered that I have to expect to find them, before I actually do.

When I first saw this French-looking pair hanging in a small shop in my home town in Canada, my mind instantly travelled back to the time I spent in France. Association is a wonderful human attribute: hearing a particular song or seeing familiar things can resurrect memories of past experiences.

Later I discovered that the artistic duo who made these masks are French Canadians whose ancestors emigrated to French Canada—which subsequently became the province of Quebec. They themselves moved to British Columbia, but this pair of masks echoes their French heritage. No matter where a person chooses to migrate, their heritage goes with them, as I saw also for my African and BC First Nations masks. In their new surroundings, the mask makers blend what they find with what they brought. The resulting cultural mix makes a beautiful tapestry illustrating the diversity of human cultures. I found that masks express this diversity.[25]

Population: 60.5 million

Capital city: Paris

People and Origins: French, North African, German, Breton, Provençal, Catalan and Basque.

Languages: French (official language), Flemish, Alsacian, Corsican, Slavic, Basque, German, Breton, North African and Indochinese.[23]

**HEAD OF MEDUSA**

Medusa, with snakes in place of hair, was said to be so hideous that a person would turn to stone from looking directly at her.

Made of fired clay

10" x 10" x 3.5"

Bought in Naxos

**ZEUS THE RULER**

Zeus is lord of the sky, the rain god. His weapon is a thunderbolt, which he hurls at those who displease him.

Made of fired clay

14.5" x 9" x 4.5"

Bought in Naxos

# Greece

Greece is the birthplace of today's modern Western society. In classical times dating back almost 3,000 years, Greece was home to three main civilizations: the Trojan civilization based in Troy, the Cretan or Minoan civilization centred on Crete, and the Helladic or Mycenaean civilization of the Greek mainland.[27] As a modern state it achieved independence from the Ottoman Empire (Turkey) in 1829.

Religion dominated Greek life in ancient times and so temples were among the largest and most elegant structures. The temples also served political purposes, including celebration of civic identity and giving thanks to patron deities for military conquests.[28]

The mythology of the Titans is entwined with Greek history, and is evident in the masks available there. The Titans were associated with the planets, many of whose names we use to this day.[29] Also referred to as the elder gods, the Titans ruled until overthrown by the Olympians.

The splendid masks of Greece usually embody its mythology. I bought the two masks opposite and the two in the Introduction on the islands of Naxos and Crete. The wooden ones from Crete were made right in the shop where I bought them.

Population: 10.5 million

Capital city: Athens

People and Origins: Greek with minorities of Albanians, Turks and Slavic-Macedonians.

Languages: Greek (official language), English, French.[26]

**WINKING MYSTIC**

I loved this mask the moment I saw it; the impressive proper eye wink is unique among my masks. I was instantly reminded of the Stanley Kubrick film *Eyes Wide Shut*.

Made of fired clay

10" x 7.5" x 4"

Bought from a street vendor in Prague

**HALLOWED DECEIVER**

This mask is as impressive as Winking Mystic. Some may think this one appears hallowed with the brass ring, but to me the look is rather one of trying to deceive.

Made of fired clay, brass

11.5" x 9" x 4"

Bought from a street vendor in Prague

# Czech Republic

The Czech Republic is one of the most stable and prosperous of the post-Communist states of Central and Eastern Europe.

The closely related Czechs and Slovaks first formed a united country in the 9th century, again in the Austro-Hungarian Empire and yet again after the First World War to form Czechoslovakia. When the Soviets lost control in 1989, Czechoslovakia peacefully won freedom through its so-called "Velvet Revolution," with no casualties. Shortly after, in January 1993, the country divided peacefully into the Czech Republic and Slovakia. The economy is now booming.[31]

The ancient city of Prague is located on the Vltava River, which is spanned by several bridges. In summer the Charles Bridge is crowded with portrait painters, vendors, buskers, tourists and pickpockets. King Charles IV ordered the start of construction for this magnificent structure in 1357,[32] and from it you can see castles on the hills above and tourists in boats moving up and down the river. On the bridge, I bought these two masks from a vendor who had made them himself (photo at right). He told me the dark shading was created by smoking the mask in burning paper before firing. The charcoal leaves a black tint.

Population: 10.27 million

Capital city: Prague

People and Origins: Czech with minorities of Slovaks, Poles, Germans, Romanies and Hungarians.

Language: Czech.[30]

**VENETIAN BLUE**

I can imagine this mask being the final complement to an ornate costume; now milady is ready for the ball.

Made of ceramic, fabric, wood, paint

21" x 6.5" x 4.5"

Bought in a discount-fashions chain store, Langley, BC

**THE ENCHANTRESS**

In the costume of the fool, with the bells, this looks to be a female, but she's no fool.

Made of brass bells, fabric, fired clay, paint

18" x 16" x 4"

Bought in a curio store, Langley, BC

# Italy

Rome was the heart of one of the world's biggest empires, which dissolved into anarchy during the Dark Ages. Italy was rejuvenated during the Renaissance, then dominated by Napoleon, and eventually became a nation-state in 1861 when various city-states united with Sardinia and Sicily. Its roller-coaster politics continued with Mussolini, and postwar frictions between extreme left and right have sometimes brought periods of chaos.[34]

I had seen the prices asked in Europe for ceramic masks like the two at left, so it was more practical to buy in Canada at half the cost. I often find that masks cost less when they are sold far away from where they were made.

Population: 57.6 million

Capital city: Rome

People and Origins: Italian

Languages: Italian and its many dialects, plus German, French and Slovene.[33]

# PACIFIC RIM

I live on the West Coast of Canada, where we are aware of our connection to the peoples of the Pacific Rim through tourism, trade and immigration.

The Pacific Rim is defined more by the Pacific Ocean than by its land areas. Some people include more countries than others. At the least it includes the small nations of eastern Asia, the West Coasts of Canada and the United States, Australia, New Zealand, the Pacific Islands, the Philippines and eastern Russia. Some people also include Mexico and Central America, and countries on the Pacific coast of South America.

My focus on masks of the Pacific Rim will be a select few countries in the northern region, although I stretch south a bit to include Hawaii.

# Hawaii

The isolated group of islands in the central Pacific Ocean known as Hawaii comprise the 50th state of the United States. Hawaii became a U.S. territory in 1900 and was admitted to the Union as a state in 1959.

We visited there in 1992. I viewed an evening dance performance and bought this mask afterward.

**FEARSOME WARRIOR**

This wooden warrior mask seems carved to be scary, with the repeated eye theme intended to put fear in the eyes of observers.

Made of wood

23.5" x 11" x 6"

Bought in the Polynesian Cultural Center, Hawaii

Population: 1.2 million

Capital city: Honolulu

People and Origins: Mulatto, Caucasian, Japanese, Filipino, Chinese, Hawaiian

Languages: English, pidgin and Hawaiian

# Hong Kong

**MR. TURTLE**

I like this mask, but wouldn't have bought it myself as I prefer to not buy endangered-species elements. The eyes are stone and the metal face elements are glued onto the shell.

Made of turtle shell, metal, stone

6" x 4" x 3.5"

A gift from Cliff, a friend

The territory of Hong Kong consists of several islands and a section of Chinese mainland. The city of Victoria is on Hong Kong Island, although the name Victoria is usually used now only for Victoria Harbour and the mountain peak overlooking the city.[35] The territory was a British colony from 1841 to 1997,[36] when it reverted to China. Many people left just before this agreement took effect, although many have since returned. It is now known as Hong Kong Special Administrative Region.[37]

Population: 6.7 million

People and Origins: Chinese, European

Languages: Cantonese, English, Mandarin and many other Asian and European languages

**JOLLY FELLOW**

This smiling face looks similar to the ones used for theatrical performances.

Made of wood, rope

9.5" x 6" x 4"

Bought in a flea market, Cloverdale, BC

**DOTTED LADY**

This mask was purchased with Jolly Fellow.

Made of wood, rope

9.5" x 6.5" x 3.5"

Bought in a flea market, Cloverdale, BC

# Japan

Japan has retained a lot of its ancient culture, thanks partly to 250 years of self-imposed isolation. It began adopting Western technology after an 1854 treaty with the United States. Japan then expanded to become a regional power, eventually defeating both Chinese and Russian forces and occupying large areas of eastern and southeastern Asia, including Manchuria and China. Its famous attack on Pearl Harbour in 1941 brought America into World War II.

Postwar Japan became a significant economy as an ally of the United States, but declined in the 1990s after three decades of growth. The emperor sits on the traditional throne, but politicians, bureaucrats and business executives have the real power.[38]

Japan is another country on my wish list to visit. The two masks at left were bought in a flea market in Cloverdale, BC, near where I live. My other Japanese mask is my smallest mask: only three inches long, but it's not in this book.

Population: 126.9 million

Capital city: Tokyo

People and Origins: Japanese, Korean, indigenous Ainu and Okinawans

Languages: Japanese

**LADY OF DISTINCTION**

The headdress feels almost like velvet to the touch. The paint is matte, not gloss.

Made of wood, paint

24" x 11" x 5"

A gift from my wife, Agnes

**FEELING BLUE**

There is great beauty here. Imagine that the dots are stars, and a galaxy glitters across the forehead.

Made of wood, paint

20" x 8" x 2"

Gift from a friend

# Thailand

The long coastline of Thailand faces both the Andaman Sea and the Gulf of Thailand in Southeast Asia. The neighbour to the north is Myanmar (Burma).

The Thai kingdom dates from the mid-14th century, and was known as Siam until 1939. A peaceful revolution in 1932 created a constitutional monarchy. Thailand was never colonized, although it was occupied by Japan during World War II. Since then it has alternated frequently between democratic and military governments.[41]

My brother Andrew and I were in Thailand for three weeks and visited Chiang Mai, where we rode the elephants. That's why I like the elephant masks, as a reminder. This is my personal version of what masks do for a culture: they evoke history, reminding people of past experiences.

Bangkok is crowded, but it's a shopper's paradise. It has everything you can possibly imagine. I saw masks almost everywhere, and the night market is something else: hundreds and hundreds of vendors stretching for blocks. Several of my Thai masks were bought there. My biggest problem was how to take them all home! I think I bought 15 masks on that trip.

Population: 62 million

Capital city: Bangkok

People and Origins: Thai, Chinese, Malay, Mon, Khmer, Phuan and Karen[39]

Languages: Thai and indigenous languages[40]

**SMILING MAIDEN**

"Land of smiles" is the motto in Thailand. Smiling Maiden reminds me of this expression.

Made of wood, cut glass

11" x 8" x 2"

Bought at the Bangkok night market

**LUCKY FROG**

My "good luck" frog! The mouth opens and closes. This is a favourite with children; they are always drawn to it.

Made of wood, paint

7" x 6" x 4"

Bought in a specialty store, Lynden, WA, USA

**THE WINKER**

I have not seen another mask like this one with the hand blocking the eye. Perhaps it's saying, "I spy, with my little eye...".

Made of wood, paint

11" x 7.5" x 1.5"

A gift from my brother David, bought at the Bangkok night market

**LONG TONGUE**

According to the vendor, this mask dates back to the 1800s. I've never seen another one resembling it.

Made of wood, leather, brass

18" x 8" x 4"

Bought in a flea market, Cloverdale, BC

**THE EXAMINER**

When I hung this on the wall at eye level I instantly had an eerie feeling, as if the mask was trying to intimidate me. I haven't had that feeling with any other mask.

Made of painted wood, bark

16" x 11" x 8"

Bought in Gastown, Vancouver, BC

# British Columbia, Canada

The federal capital of Canada is Ottawa, and Canada's population totals 32.8 million. The country's ethnic diversity has strong regional differences. For example, British influence is stronger in BC than in other provinces.

The indigenous First Nations people of the Pacific Northwest have lived and flourished here for over ten thousand years, since the end of the last Ice Age. Western archaeologists believe that these First Nations groups have been here since 9,000 BC.

The land and sea produced plenty of food and raw material, and let them develop complex societies and the complex art forms that are now internationally famous. For example, the Haida nation who live on the beautiful islands in northern BC (known for a time as the Queen Charlotte Islands and now, again, as Haida Gwaii) are noted for their skilled artisans.

The modern history of the Canadian province of British Columbia can be dated from 1794, when the first whites settled at Fort St. John. The London-based Hudson's Bay Company (HBC) opened its first trading post at Hudson's Hope in the North in 1805, and built Fort Victoria on Vancouver Island in 1843. The colony of

Population: 4.1 million

Capital city: Victoria

People and Origins: European, Asian, East Indian, "First Nations" indigenous groups

Languages: English, French, Cantonese, Mandarin, indigenous languages, numerous Asian and other immigrant languages

**KOMOKWA**

Komokwa is king of the undersea world and the protector of seals who ruled from a large house under the water.[46] His name means "the wealthy one." This myth is from the Kwakiutl tribe (information from artist).

Made of painted wood, fibre

10.5" x 8" x 4"

Bought in a flea market, Cloverdale, BC

**BOOKWUS**

The Bookwus, or Wildman of the Woods, is particularly important for the Kwakiutl tribe. This nonhuman creature lived in a ghost forest and tried to lure people to it. Spirits of the drowned were attracted to his invisible home (information from artist).

Made of painted wood

11.5" x 9.5" x 6.5"

Bought in a flea market, Cloverdale, BC

Vancouver Island was established in 1849 when the entire island was leased by First Nations to the HBC.

In addition to the natural wealth of the area that First Nations enjoyed, as manifested in their possessions and potlatches, great monetary wealth arrived from their trade with Europeans in fur and salmon. Although the natives were, in general, fairly well treated by the Hudson's Bay Company, the settlers' arrival had negative consequences too. As elsewhere, colonial contact introduced native people to guns, alcohol and diseases.[42]

## First Nations of British Columbia: Masks and Mythology

There are several different language families among the First Nations of the Pacific Northwest coast. Some are spoken by single nations or tribes, others are spoken by several tribes. The nations speaking the diverse groups of languages also developed diverse cultures. Masks are frequently used in their complex beliefs and rituals.

Different types of masks represent many aspects of their society, environment and beliefs: everything from mythical creatures to animals to humans. For example, the Beaver Totem mask (page 60) shows a beaver and a dragonfly; people linked the two because they both live in the swamps. A sea monster appears below the fin at the top. The Bookwus mask, on the other hand (left), shows a mythical creature, a ghostly cold presence who tried to get people to eat his food. If they did, they had to go and live with him. Bookwus' house was invisible, but if everything seemed cold and damp, people could tell they were near it. The spirits of the drowned were drawn to his home. The Komokwa mask (left) represents the ruler of the sea, who was associated with loons, seals and killer whales.

In many indigenous cultures, masks represent sacred spirits and ancestors brought to life for the well-being of a community. Almost always they are used to strengthen the living.[43] Among First Nations people of BC, many masks convey a magical transformation from animal to human. These masks open to reveal successive hidden masks inside. It was believed that masks made the spirit world visible.[44]

Masks made by First Nations carvers in BC differ greatly in quality. Many people try their hand at it. Wood and tools are easily available, there is no formal training system and people learn skills and myths from friends and family. Some people find they like carving. They may continue and develop a high degree of skill and achieve international status, not only in masks but other more three-dimensional objects. Others may carve only a few items as beginners and then move on to other activities.

**WOOLLY EYES**

I bought this at an antique store that was closing. The year —"1992"—and the carver's name—"Dallas Manson"—are found on the back of the mask, but this is not a known West Coast First Nations name.[48]

Made of fur, wood, paint

7" x 6" x 4"

Bought in an antique store, Langley, BC

Other things also affect the masks found here. Some First Nations people come to BC from the Prairies and eastern Canada and bring with them their cultural traditions and ideas. These artists mix with local people and learn new skills. As the owner of one local crafts shop said, "Occasionally the carvers are not from this coast, but learn the style because there is a greater demand for it, and a demand for artists skilled in it too."[45]

Some of my masks show signs of this mixing of styles and traditions. The First Nations communities of BC are small, and owners of the large stores that stock native art say they do not recognize the names of the makers of my masks, except for one, yet most are carved in the style of the West Coast. So it seems that the makers were not born and raised in the West Coast traditions.

The carver of three of my masks supplied a short explanation of the mythology on cards attached to the masks; the myths come from different tribes. The mythology of the other masks was not available when I bought them. This is not unusual. Not all carvers give the history of their masks, or even sign them. They assume that everyone knows the story. That's why I've given my own names to some of them—it is part of the way I came to own them. Even the high-quality masks seen in the Vancouver galleries that sell for many thousands of dollars do not always have the carver's name or the mythology. It is just that some carvers want to give this detail while others do not.

Masks are sold in many places in BC: galleries, auction houses, antique stores, curio shops and craft and flea markets. Often, at flea markets, the sellers don't know the value of the mask they are selling. This provides great opportunities for collectors.

The most important way to learn about masks is to go and look at them. By looking at hundreds of masks you learn to see what makes a good mask: depth of carving, good design and careful finishing. But most important of all is the spirit and energy it conveys. Ask yourself, how does it make you feel? That's what I do.

**GREEN WARRIOR**

I first saw this mask, and the next one, hanging in an Indian art store. When the shop went bankrupt, a pawnshop purchased the entire inventory. I got both masks at a very good price.

Made of wood, paint, leather

11" x 9" x 6"

Bought in a pawnshop, Langley, BC

**YELLOW BRAVE**

This mask is almost identical to its green mate. Both masks have the carver and year as "N. Elias 1998". This is not a known West Coast First Nations name.[49]

Made of wood, paint, leather

11" x 9" x 6"

Bought in a pawnshop, Langley, BC

**TRICKY RAVEN**

This mask shows a typical combination of human and bird features. It has movement: a string is pulled and the mouth opens. Ravens were part of a mythological population at the dawn of the world.[47]

Made of bark, wood, paint, string

5.5" x 14" x 4.5"

Bought in a flea market, Cloverdale, BC

**SMILING NATIVE**

This native is proud of his healthy teeth. Could this be the result of eating so much fish?

Made of fired clay, paint

9.5" x 6.75" x 3"

Bought in a flea market, Cloverdale, BC

**BEAVER TOTEM**

This mask, worn on the forehead, is based on Haida myth. The beaver, holding a chewing stick, has his tail curled up between his legs. Above the tail is a dragonfly, which also lives in the swamps. [Information on card by artist "J. Wolf"]

Made of painted wood, fibre

12" x 6.5" x 3.5"

Bought in a flea market, Cloverdale, BC

**SISTER WOLF**

This is not the northern West Coast style, and might not have been made by a First Nations artist. A craft store owner speculated that it might be from the southern West Coast, or what he called "New Age Native."[50]

Made of feathers, fired clay

10" x 7" x 4"

Bought in a ceramics store, White Rock, BC

**FUR FACE**

The wrinkled expression gives life-like character to this native. This may be Inuit, more commonly known as Eskimo.

Made of ceramic, fur

5.5" x 4" x 1.5"

Bought in a souvenir store, Juneau, AK

The long house at Skidegate, Haida Gwaii/Queen Charlotte Islands, British Columbia. It is presently used as a school to teach and preserve the Haida language. The totem pole was made by Bill Reid, the most famous First Nations carver in Canada, and erected in 1978. 2005
*– G. Dahl*

# Reconnection

## Turning Back to Tradition

As my collection grew, I learned that mask makers around the world are losing their traditional cultures. So I wondered what now inspires these carvers. Although I began collecting masks in other countries, I found the answer in BC where I live. Here, the living First Nations tradition shows how mask makers are helping to preserve culture.

Just two events enlightened me quickly. First, I met a very skilled—and hospitable—mask maker, who was willing to answer my questions. I was intrigued, like seeing inside a watch and wondering how it works. I found that Reg Davidson was an expert carver and a reliable source of information. He kindly allowed me an interview in a park in Vancouver.

Second, he invited Agnes and me to visit his ancestral home at Masset, on the northern tip of Graham Island, one of the Queen Charlotte Islands (known locally as Haida Gwaii) off the coast of northern BC. We took a day trip down to Skidegate in the south of Graham Island, to attend a most important ceremony for First Nations. This occasion showed me that indigenous people can reverse the processes that weaken their cultures.

Reg Davidson
*— Bruce Stotesbury, 2005. Victoria Times-Colonist*

### A First Nations Mask Carver

Reg Davidson is a third-generation Haida artist, born in 1954 in Masset, Haida Gwaii (Queen Charlotte Islands), BC. He has achieved international acclaim as a sculptor and mask carver. Reg is also an accomplished dancer and singer with the Rainbow Creek Dancers, a Haida dance group that he and his brother Robert formed in 1980. Reg made a lot of the group's equipment, including masks, drums, and kid-leather dance capes.[51]

# Interview with Reg Davidson[52]

*What do you hope to convey with your carvings?*

At one time all of our art had a purpose or meaning or function. But there is no word for art in our language. It took me a long time to understand that a mask does not need to have a function, such as when I make a headpiece that does not fit on anyone's head. The art is when I make one for myself and use it for dance. I do this for others—they can enjoy it, even if they do not know anything about masks or dance. I help them understand our culture. I want them to enjoy it, even without knowing our history.

*What is your process in selecting, painting and forming the image of your masks?*

Someone asked me once, what is the best piece I've carved. I did not know how to answer him. I asked another carver and he said to me, "Well, maybe it is because, when you carve, you are thinking about your next piece." For me it takes sometimes two or three attempts to make one piece. My hands don't seem to cooperate with me sometimes (laughs), and it does not become the image I have in my mind. So my last carving brings me to my next piece. Yes, it is a progression.

We used to make our own paint, but not anymore. I like using red and black. Sometimes I will use red, say for the nose, and add another red in subtleties, to see if people notice what I have done.

*Are certain woods used for different purposes? Does one wood have more power than others?*

For a lot of masks I use red cedar for its lightness, mostly because of dance. Birch and maple are hard, but too heavy. I use maple or birch for making rattles. Because they are harder, they give different sounds. If I want more detail then I use an alder, since it is so soft, like carving with cork. If I want a real fine detail, I use yellow cedar.

*Is there a spiritual significance in the kind of wood you use?*

Not for me. But if there is spiritual significance, red cedar is the backbone of our art. Our longhouses were made from red cedar, our hats were also made of red cedar, and so for our culture to survive, we need red cedar. I am sure many people don't know that.

*Have you ever experienced a feeling from a mask? To give you an example of my own experience, when I hung a West Coast warrior mask,*

Reg Davidson using a rotating vise and calipers in carving a moon mask from red cedar.

*— Dr. Carol Ventura, http://iweb.tntech.edu/cventura/reg.htm*

*I was eye to eye with it. It was as if the eyes were looking straight into me. That very instant I had a feeling run down my spine. It was quite a shock. Even now I get this feeling when I look at it. When you carve a mask, do you ever get an energy or feeling from it?*

I do—only when I am dancing, when I use it. When I use something I have created, I give it life. It all depends on what I am using it for, like maybe a mask used in a ceremony.

*Is there a difference between ceremonial masks for weddings, funerals or coming of age?*

They are much the same. A mask comes alive when I use it in dance.

*Is that because you created it?*

Well, like, now I get this piece of wood and I start to carve. I don't draw it out first. I see the image and carve till something happens—just like that!

*With transformation masks, does the spirit of an ancestor or animal enter the person?*

I can give one example. When my dad died, we had an End of Mourning dance (performed a year after the person died). I used all of my dad's regalia, and when I danced I became him. It was very powerful! I had this feeling come all over me. After I had used it, I was exhausted and I started to cry. I knew it was an energy more than just mine, someone else's too, I don't know if it was Dad or not, I just felt that it was.

*So was it like a spiritual deposit from the individual in the costume and mask?*

Yes it was.

*Are there certain masks that are never sold? Are some used only once and destroyed?*

Yes, the End of Mourning ones used for dance—like the one I used for my sister's—I burned. Also, the very first mask I made for the longhouse. I made a frog one, and I burned that one also. There are some masks that are made and are not sold, but that's not what I do. Anything I make, I want to be used or enjoyed.

*Are there some masks that are evil or good?*

I think it depends on who is wearing it—I don't know.

*Well, are there some masks used for evil purposes, like in ceremonies?*

Well I don't think the mask is evil, maybe it looks scary, but it is useful. It may be that it just shows our own fear, what we have inside.

*For you, carving seems more than a business. So what legacy would you like to leave with your work, say when you depart this earthly dimension?*

Carvings completed by Reg Davidson in 2003: drum, platters, clogs and masks. Note the handles in front of the masks that are used to make parts move.

*— Dr. Carol Ventura,*
*http://iweb.tntech.edu/cventura/reg.htm*

*If someone sees your work, what story would you like it to tell?*

I would like to be one of the people that helps put our culture back together. No one does this alone. I just want to do my part. I am just one of many—I would like to be a stepping-stone bringing our culture back, like our singing and dancing. Giving this to my grand-children. And my carvings and dance are a part of this that I would like to instil in others.

They say our culture is dying, but as long as there is a Haida living then our culture is still alive. But we adapt, just as the world is changing. We evolve like everyone else. So it is not like we are losing our culture, we are just evolving.

*So would you like to have your son carve? Do you think carving is a gift?*

Carving requires discipline, but many people do not have discipline. Like sports, carving looks easy. But no one sees the hours that sports players practise. It is all discipline.

Garth and Agnes Dahl with Reg Davidson.
*— G. Dahl*

Haida families go out to the kelp beds to scatter flowers, in the End of Mourning ceremony at Skidegate, 2005.
*— G. Dahl*

# The End of Mourning

I first met and interviewed Reg Davidson in Vancouver, BC, but experiencing another culture happens best when immersed in it, as I found when I visited him in Masset. Books and pictures can orient you to another culture, but they cannot compare to visiting people on home territory. Agnes and I stayed with Reg and his family for a week, and got acquainted with them and local culture.

It was strange at first to be outsiders in a small community, but Reg's family were very welcoming and we ate with them like friends. Agnes helped Reg's aunt sew buttons on a button blanket for a ceremonial costume. In the wider community we were still strangers, and I started to realize that not many outsiders experience the personal connection that we enjoyed. I had heard that wariness exists between many First Nations people and white people, and saw how easy it would be to fall into that trap of distrust.

We enjoyed a personal connection—and a lot more. Our visit coincided with a historic event that gave me a unique experience of First Nations culture. I was one of a few fortunate outsiders to witness this event. The memories of such moments last a lifetime, and I will cherish them deeply. On the morning of June 21, 2005, National Aboriginal Day and the summer solstice, Agnes and I took part in a ceremony of repatriation on Skidegate Beach in Haida Gwaii: the ritual known as End of Mourning.

From the late 1800s, after smallpox had almost wiped out the Haida, anthropologists and private collectors took thousands of artifacts and bones from Haida burial sites. For decades these objects and the bones of Haida ancestors were displayed and studied in museums in America, Britain and Europe. Many remains and artifacts are still in private collections.

For the last ten years the Haida have struggled to have these objects repatriated, and many remains and items have been returned, notably by curators at the Canadian Museum of Civilization in Gatineau, Quebec, the American Museum of Natural History in New York City, the Field Museum in Chicago, the University of Oregon, the Department of Archaeology at Simon Fraser University, the Oakland Museum of California, and the Laboratory of Archaeology at the University of British Columbia in Vancouver. Museums in Europe and Britain have yet to cooperate. [53]

This struggle is a major clash of values between the Haida on one hand, and scientists, anthropologists and museum curators on the other. As in many traditional cultures, the Haida believe that if their bones are removed from their homeland, the spirits of the dead cannot rest. Curators say that valuable artifacts would decay if not preserved, while scientists want to study DNA for clues to human migration and the evolution of diseases.[54]

Haida men carry bentwood chests to be given as gifts to different Haida clans at the End of Mourning feast. — *G. Dahl*

In ceremonial dress: Chief Niis Wes (Ernie Wilson), left, and Chief Skidegate (Clarence Dempsey Collinson). — *G. Dahl*

The repatriation ceremony marked the end of mourning for more than 460 ancestors, whose remains had been repatriated and reburied over the past ten years, as they were brought home from different museums. The ceremony was held also for those who died from smallpox and other epidemics.[55]

The End of Mourning ceremony is a rite of passage, the final ceremony for a deceased person. It is usually held after at least one year of mourning. Headstones are placed to mark the grave, and/or memorial poles are raised. Prayers are said, and an offering of food is made, to honour the spirits of the deceased and allow them to depart peacefully to "the other side," or the Spirit Land.[56]

On this day, several hundred people, both natives and outsiders like us, gathered on the beach around fires. Wearing ceremonial dress, the family members of the repatriated arrived, bringing traditional foods. Some they threw into the fire as offerings.

Then members of the families said prayers or sang. When the ceremony had ended, spectators were asked if they wanted to offer a blessing. I felt inclined to participate, yet I felt reserved—an outsider at a ceremony in a different culture—even though we had spent a week with Reg and his family. But I wanted to identify with the families and share their experience.

Many white people there were standing a little distance away. Those who came closer got more

Leaders of the Haida community and guests at the ceremonial fire, Skidegate, 2005.
*— G. Dahl*

of the feeling of the event. Agnes and I stepped forward, and it was like crossing a bridge; I felt out of my comfort zone. An elder gave us offerings of tobacco. As I threw mine on the fire,

Haida men in traditional dress at the End of Mourning ceremony. — *G. Dahl*

I prayed that this ceremony would heal the years of pain, and not only give rest to the departed, but also bring peace to those who remain. I felt very sombre, and realized I was no longer just observing: I was participating. I thought that maybe I felt a bit of how they were feeling. It was very moving. Then we went up the hill and everyone ate a little.

After a while the families went down to the dock, got into longboats and paddled back over towards us on the nearby shore, bringing traditional bentwood boxes. These they took up to the cemetery, where they were given to families of the deceased. We watched from outside.

Then the families went out in the boats again, scattered flowers on the water over the kelp beds, and returned to the shore. That ended the formal part of the ceremony. In the evening there was feasting, celebration and spirit dances, continuing long after we left. Now the Haida ancestors can rest in peace.

I wondered afterward how I would feel if my family's bones were the ones that had been stolen and examined. The very thought disturbed me, and it was eye-opening: as though I was seeing the world more through native eyes, less through my white eyes. Seeing myself as the victim, for a change, quickly affected my understanding. Part of me had not wanted to participate, and for me to step forward was hard. But I just had to take the first step. Then it was easy to walk.

The ceremonial fire, on which offerings of food and tobacco were thrown during the End of Mourning ceremony.

— *G. Dahl*

## Conclusion

Masks are simple but powerful expressions of culture found all over the world. In the past they were crafted for special ceremonies and rituals; today many masks are made for the marketplace. We hang them on our walls, we see them displayed in galleries and museums and we wear them in special ceremonies. Masks continue to fascinate us with their ties to ancient civilizations and mystical beliefs.

When I first saw masks on my travels, I collected them for their unique materials, vivid colours and interesting facial expressions. Later I began to see masks as an important aspect of world culture, whether people make them for a living or for their community and rituals. When I encountered the First Nations masks of British Columbia, I came to know some of the history and folklore of their origins, and began to appreciate their value as faces of cultural history. My book does not show the full range of masks found around the world, nor did I set out, like a museum collector, to make a representative sample of masks in any particular country or region. Yet, when I think of what I could find in Australia, New Guinea, China or Russia, I get the urge to travel again.

Collecting masks has taught me to look at the world and its people more closely. I believe this book will have the same effect on you. Whether you are inspired to begin a collection yourself or learn more about masks and other native art 0 the ancient—and contemporary—cultures of our world.

*— Garth Dahl*

# References


1. Bruce Kirkland, "Hayden Goes over to the Dark Side," Jam! Showbiz: Movies, Toronto Sun in Sun Media Newspapers/Canoe Quebecor Media, http://jam.canoe.ca/Movies/2005/05/15/1040791.html (accessed May 15, 2005).

2. Lonely Planet Publications Pty Ltd., Travelocity.co.uk, http://www.travelocity.co.uk/TEU_destGuide/0,,TCYUK|14036|1611,00.html (accessed November 6, 2005).

3. Expediciones Tropicales, "Costa Rica History," Costa Rica Guides, http://www.costaricaguides.com/costa_rica_history_.html (accessed March 18, 2005).

4. op. cit.

5. Encyclopaedia Britannica, "History of the Mask: Preservation and Collecting," AnyMask.com and ABM Mask & Costume Enterprises Inc., http://www.anymask.com/historyofmask.html (accessed March 18, 2005).

6. Lonely Planet Publications Pty Ltd., "Cuba," Travelocity.co.uk, http://www.travelocity.co.uk/TEU_destGuide/0,,TCYUK|14036|1623,00.html (accessed November 6, 2005).

7. Cubatravel.cu, "¿What does Cuba means?" Publicitur S.A., http://www.cubatravel.cu/client/information/cuba.php?locale=en (accessed March 18, 2005).

8. EduToursToCuba.com, "About Cuba: History," Voyage Culture Cuba Inc., http://www.edutourstocuba.com/cuba/cuba_hist.html (accessed March 18, 2005).

9. The Applied History Research Group, "The European Voyages of Exploration: The Conquest Of The Aztec Empire: Hernán Cortés," The University of Calgary, http://www.ucalgary.ca/applied_history/tutor/eurvoya/aztec.html (accessed March 19, 2005).

10. FOCUS SOUTH Consulting, "Cuba In Brief," Doing Business With Cuba, http://www.travelnet.com/~blochfd/brief.html (accessed March 19, 2005).

11. Lonely Planet Publications Pty Ltd., "México," Travelocity.co.uk, http://www.travelocity.co.uk/TEU_destGuide/0,,TCYUK|14036|3471,00.html (accessed November 6, 2005).

12. The Canadian Society for Mesoamerican Studies, "The Aztecs," Canadian University Programmes: Cultures of Mesoamerica, http://www.csms.ca/Aztec%20Culture.htm (accessed March 19, 2005).

13. The Applied History Research Group, "The European Voyages of Exploration: The Conquest Of The Aztec Empire: Hernán Cortés," University of Calgary,http://www.ucalgary.ca/applied_history/tutor/eurvoya/aztec.html (accessed November 6, 2005).

14. http://www.csms.ca/Aztec%20Culture.htm op.cit.

15. Lonely Planet Publications Pty Ltd., "Brazil," Travelocity.co.uk, http://www.travelocity.co.uk/TEU_destGuide/0,,TCYUK|14036|5232,00.html (accessed November 6, 2005).

16. Lonely Planet Publications Pty Ltd., "Brazil—History," Travelocity.co.uk, http://www.travelocity.co.uk/TEU_destGuide/0,4179,TCYUK|14036|5232|322|1,00.html

17. Original Diamonds.com, "A layer of crystals that form within a mineral crust," Jewelry & Gem Dictionary, http://www.original-diamonds.com/dictionary_d.php

18. From a card attached to the mask. Properties of the stones are listed as follows:

*Amethyst—Creates peace of mind and brings good luck.*

*Agate—Increases strength and protection and support.*

*Citrine—Aids in creating a strong physical image.*

*Red Jasper—Increases the body's metabolism.*

*Zebra Jasper—Influences security and stability.*

*Green Jasper—Promotes your well being.*

*Crystal Quartz—Strengthens your aura, balances emotions and stimulates your brain.*

*Rose Quartz—Calms your spirit, banishes fears and reduces pain.*

*Blue Quartz—Provides energy and calms the mind.*

*Green quartz—Increases your luck, purifies your mind.*

*Sodalite—Dispels guilt and fears, aids in clearing the mind.*

19. Massa, Richard W., "The Africa I Know," The Harry and Berniece Gockel International Symposium, 1998, http://www.mssu.edu/international/africa/afriknow.htm (accessed March 19, 2005).

20. Douglas Curran, personal communication to editor, June 23, 2005. He has photographed mask rituals in Malawi and elsewhere.

21. Lonely Planet Publications Pty Ltd., "Ghana," Travelocity.co.uk, http://www.travelocity.co.uk/TEU_destGuide/0,,TCYUK|1|351,00.html (accessed November 6, 2005).

22. InterKnowledge Corp., "An Introduction to Africa: Exploring Ghana," http://www.geographia.com/ghana/ (accessed March 19, 2005).

23. Lonely Planet Publications Pty Ltd., "France," Travelocity.co.uk, http://www.travelocity.co.uk/TEU_destGuide/0,,TCYUK|1762|1866,00.html

24. Lonely Planet Publications Pty Ltd., "France—History," Travelocity.co.uk, http://www.travelocity.co.uk/TEU_destGuide/0,4179,TCYUK|1762|1866|3407|1,00.html; (accessed November 3, 2005).

25. The work of Georges Gamache and Micheline Larose, well-known in Canada, portrays French-Canadian experience. Some of their work is in museums, for example "Voyageur puppet" in the St. Boniface Museum in Manitoba, also on The Virtual Museum of Canada, run by the federal Department of Canadian Heritage: http://www.virtualmuseum.ca/Exhibitions/Gestes/anglais/r_a_msb.html

26. Lonely Planet Publications Pty Ltd., "Greece," Travelocity.co.uk, http://www.travelocity.co.uk/TEU_destGuide/0,,TCYUK|1762|2039,00.html (accessed November 6, 2005).

27. Kästle, Klaus (Editor), "Greece," Nations Online Project, http://www.nationsonline.org/oneworld/greece.htm (accessed March 19, 2005).

28. AncientGreece.com, "Architecture in Ancient Greece," World News Network/United Artists Inc., http://www.ancientgreece.com/art/art.htm (accessed March 19, 2005).

29. John M. Hunt, "The Titans," Greek Mythology, http://edweb.sdsu.edu/people/bdodge/scaffold/GG/titan.html (accessed March 19, 2005).

30. Lonely Planet Publications Pty Ltd., "Czech Republic," Travelocity.co.uk, http://www.travelocity.co.uk/TEU_destGuide/0,,TCYUK|1762|1813,00.html (accessed November 6, 2005).

31. Lonely Planet Publications Pty Ltd., "Czech Republic—History," Travelocity.co.uk, http://www.travelocity.co.uk/TEU_destGuide/0,4179,TCYUK|1762|1813|3137|1,00.html (accessed November 6, 2005).

32. Wikipedia: the Free Encyclopedia, "Charles Bridge," http://en.wikipedia.org/wiki/Charles_Bridge (accessed November 6, 2005).

33. Lonely Planet Publications Pty Ltd., "Italy," Travelocity.co.uk, http://www.travelocity.co.uk/TEU_destGuide/0,,TCYUK|1762|2121,00.html (accessed November 6, 2005).

34. Lonely Planet Publications Pty Ltd., "Italy—History," Travelocity.co.uk, http://www.travelocity.co.uk/TEU_destGuide/0,4179,TCYUK|1762|2121|3786|1,00.html (accessed November 6, 2005).

35. Wikipedia: the Free Encyclopedia, "Victoria City," http://en.wikipedia.org/wiki/Victoria_City (accessed November 6, 2005).

36. Lonely Planet Publications Pty Ltd., "Hong Kong—History," Travelocity.co.uk, http://www.travelocity.co.uk/TEU_destGuide/0,4179,TCYUK|794|2771|806|1,00.html (accessed November 6, 2005).

37. Wikipedia: the Free Encyclopedia, "Hong Kong," http://en.wikipedia.org/wiki/Hong_Kong (accessed November 6, 2005).

38. Lonely Planet Publications Pty Ltd., "Japan—History," Travelocity.co.uk, http://www.travelocity.co.uk/TEU_destGuide/0,4179,TCYUK|794|2662|922|1,00.html (accessed November 6, 2005).

39. Lonely Planet Publications Pty Ltd., "Thailand," Travelocity.co.uk, http://www.travelocity.co.uk/TEU_destGuide/0,,TCYUK|794|5942,00.html (accessed November 6, 2005).

40. Wikipedia: the Free Encyclopedia, "Demographics of Thailand," http://en.wikipedia.org/wiki/Demographics_of_Thailand (accessed November 6, 2005).

41. Lonely Planet Publications Pty Ltd., "Thailand—History," Travelocity.co.uk, http://www.travelocity.co.uk/TEU_destGuide/0,4179,TCYUK|794|5942|2088|1,00.html (accessed November 6, 2005).

42. British Columbia.com, "History and Heritage of British Columbia, Canada," Shangaan Webservices Incorporated, http://www.britishcolumbia.com/general/details.asp?id=22 (accessed March 19, 2005).

43. Curious Masks, "About Curious Masks," http://curiousmasks.com/6606/information.php?info_id=3 (accessed May 17, 2005).

44. Free Spirit Gallery, "West Coast Indian Art Tribal Masks," http://www.freespiritgallery.ca/nwart-masks.htm (accessed May 17, 2005).

45. Tim Strang, marketing manager for a large Vancouver store that sells First Nations crafts, personal communication, June 27, 2005.

46. Native-Online, "Legends: Komokwa," http://www.nativeonline.com/legends.html#Komokwa (accessed May 17, 2005).

47. Native-Online, "Legends: Wren mask," http://www.nativeonline.com/legends.html (accessed May 17, 2005).

48. Tim Strang, op. cit.

49. op. cit.

50. op. cit.

51. Dr. Carol Ventura, "Reg Davidson: Haida Artist," Department of Music and Art, Tennessee Technological University, http://iweb.tntech.edu/cventura/reg.htm (accessed May 17, 2005).

52. Author's taped interview with Reg Davidson, March 2005. This is an edited transcript.

53. Information from Nika Collison, Curator, Haida Gwaii Museum, Co-chair Haida Repatriation Committee: personal email to editor, March 31, 2006.

54. Miro Cernetig, "Haida to bring home ancestors' bones," Monday, September 16, 2002, The Globe and Mail at Indian Burial and Sacred Grounds Watch, "News Items," http://www.ibsgwatch.imagedjinn.com/learn/2002sept16haida.htm (accessed November 10, 2005).

55. Information from Nika Collison, op. cit.

56. Information from Nika Collison, op. cit.

# Additional Photography Credits

v. Forest at entrance to the Tow Hill National Park, Old Masset, Haida Gwaii/Queen Charlotte Islands, BC, 2005; Garth Dahl.

viii: Six unfinished masks, workshop of Reg Davidson, Old Masset, Haida Gwaii/Queen Charlotte Islands, BC, 2005; Reg Davidson.

xvi. Facing page 1: Iguanas on Manuel Antonio Beach, Costa Rica, 2005; Garth Dahl.

3. Hammock and palm trees, Playa Tambor, Costa Rica, 2003; Garth Dahl.

3. Palm trees and ginger flowers, Los Delfines, Costa Rica, 2003; Garth Dahl.

9. Top: Dancing, Old Havana, Cuba, 2002; Garth Dahl.

9. Bottom: Shopping in Old Havana, Cuba, 2002; Garth Dahl.

15. The Pyramid of Quetzalcoatl, two views, Chichén Itzá, Mexico, 1999; Garth Dahl.

19. Coconuts at Botafogo Beach, Rio de Janeiro, Brazil, 1997; Agnes Dahl.

21. Giraffe resting by a thorn tree, Central Africa, undated; Tom Morrison.

32. Arc de Triomphe du Carrousel, Paris, 1998; Steve Jay.

33. Tower of Notre-Dame Cathedral, Paris, April 1997; Garth Dahl.

37. Top: The Acropolis, Athens, 2004; Garth Dahl.

37. Bottom: Theater of Herod Atticus, near The Acropolis, Athens, 2004; Garth Dahl.

39. Garth and mask vendor, Charles Bridge, Prague, Czech Republic, 2003; Agnes Dahl.

41. Top: Coliseum, Rome, 1998; Garth Dahl.

41. Bottom: Monument to Victor Emmanuel, Rome, 1998; Garth Dahl.

43. Facing: Tow Hill, Graham Island, Haida Gwaii/ Queen Charlotte Islands, 2005; Garth Dahl.

44. Windsurfers on Maui, 2003; Neall Calvert.

45. Victoria City, Hong Kong, undated; Kan Kin Lam.

47. Top: Tsukuba, Japan, 2004; Ewart Blackmore.

47. Bottom: Courtyard, Kyoto, Japan, 1992; Jo Blackmore.

49. Garth Dahl with two Thai women performers, Bangkok,Thailand, April 2000; Andrew Dahl.

53. Isoullock Peak, near Hope, BC, 2005; Neall Calvert.

53. Bottom: Sunset near Tow Hill, Haida Gwaii/ Queen Charlotte Islands, 2005; Garth Dahl.

# Suggested Reading on Masks


*Visions of the North: Native Art of the Northwest Coast*

Don and Debra McQuiston; text by Lynn Bush; photography by Tom Till.

Chronicle Books, 1995.

*Haida Gwaii: Journeys Through the Queen Charlotte Islands*

Text by Ian Gill; photography by David Nunuk.

Raincoast Books, 1997.

*In the Spirit of Mother Earth: Nature in Native American Art*

Text by Jeremy Schmidt; captions by Laine Thom.

Chronicle Books, 1994.

*Spirit Faces: Contemporary Masks of the Northwest Coast*

Gary Wyatt.

Douglas & McIntyre, 1994.

*Haida Monumental Art: Villages of the Queen Charlotte Islands*

George F. MacDonald.

University of British Columbia Press, 1983.

*During My Time: Florence Edenshaw Davidson, A Haida Woman*

Margaret B. Blackman.

University of Washington Press; Douglas & McIntyre, 1982.

*Myths & Legends of the Haida Indians of the Northwest: The Children of the Raven*

Martine J. Reid.

Bellerophon Books, 1991.


## Invitation to Mask Makers

It is my most sincere desire to obtain permission, as well as information, about the work of the mask makers, for subsequent editions of this book. It is also my hope that this book may serve to publicize mask makers and their work by awakening interest in readers about their craft.

Masks are usually not signed by their makers, and so it has not been possible to contact makers to request permission to include photos in this edition. Mask makers should please contact me if they find their mask(s) in my book, at masksofworld@hotmail.com or Granville Island Publishing, 212–1656 Duranleau, Vancouver, BC, Canada V6H 3S4 www.GranvilleIslandPublishing.com

*Garth Dahl — Author*

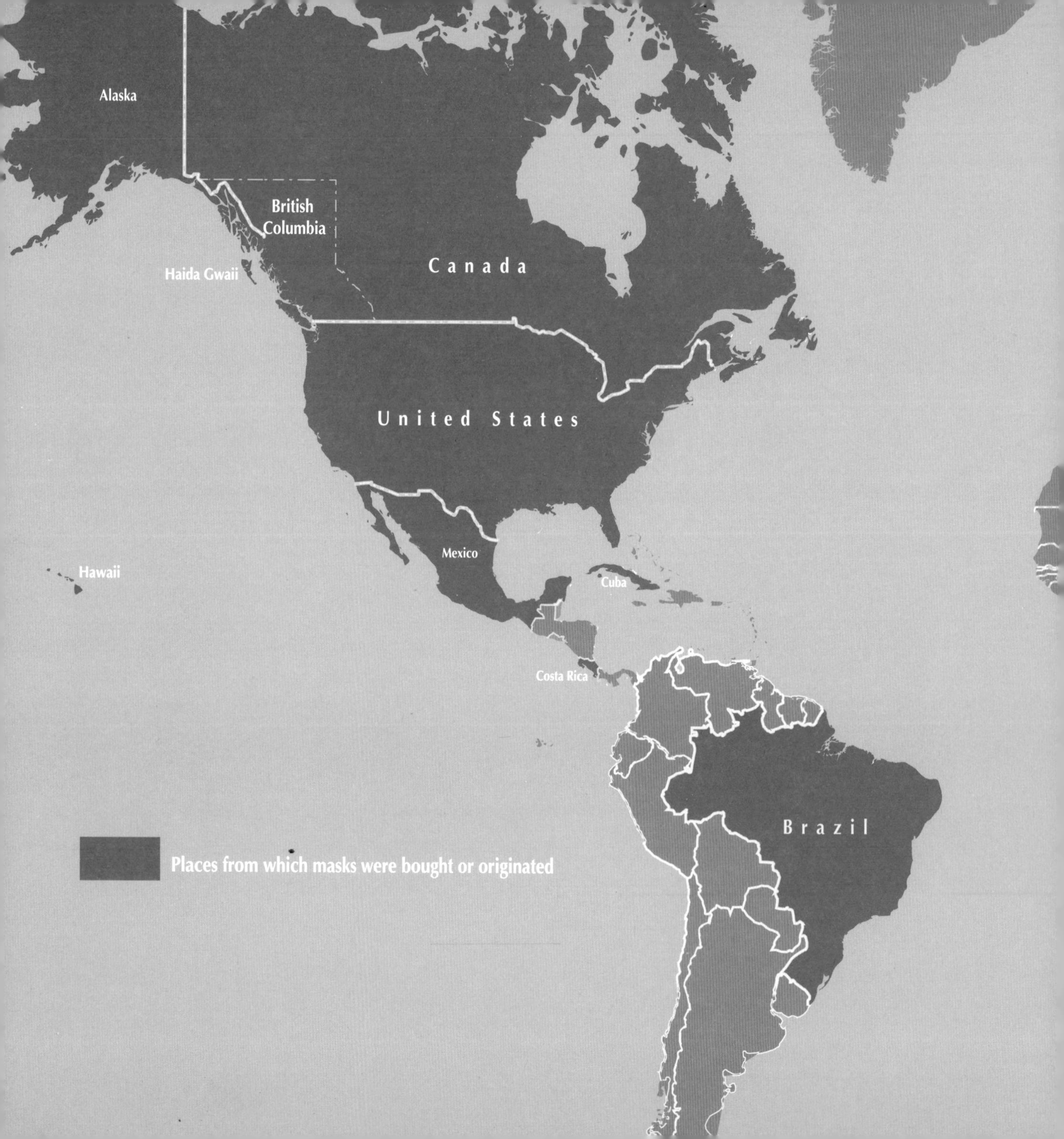
Alaska
British Columbia
Haida Gwaii
Canada
United States
Mexico
Hawaii
Cuba
Costa Rica
Brazil
Places from which masks were bought or originated